A STRESS RELIEF COLORING BOOK

DREAM
CATCHER

VOL.2

COLOR TEST PAGE

COLOR TEST PAGE

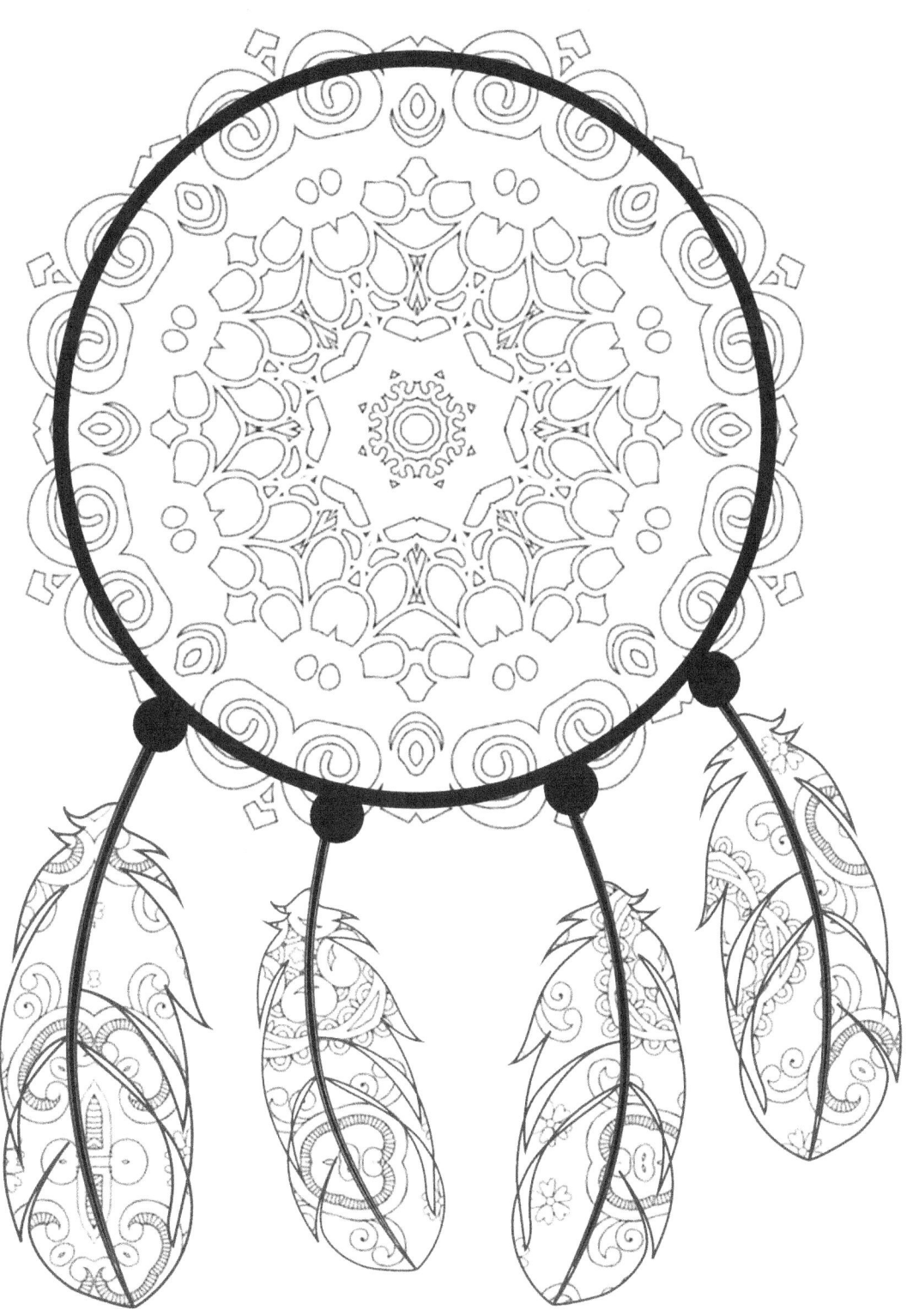

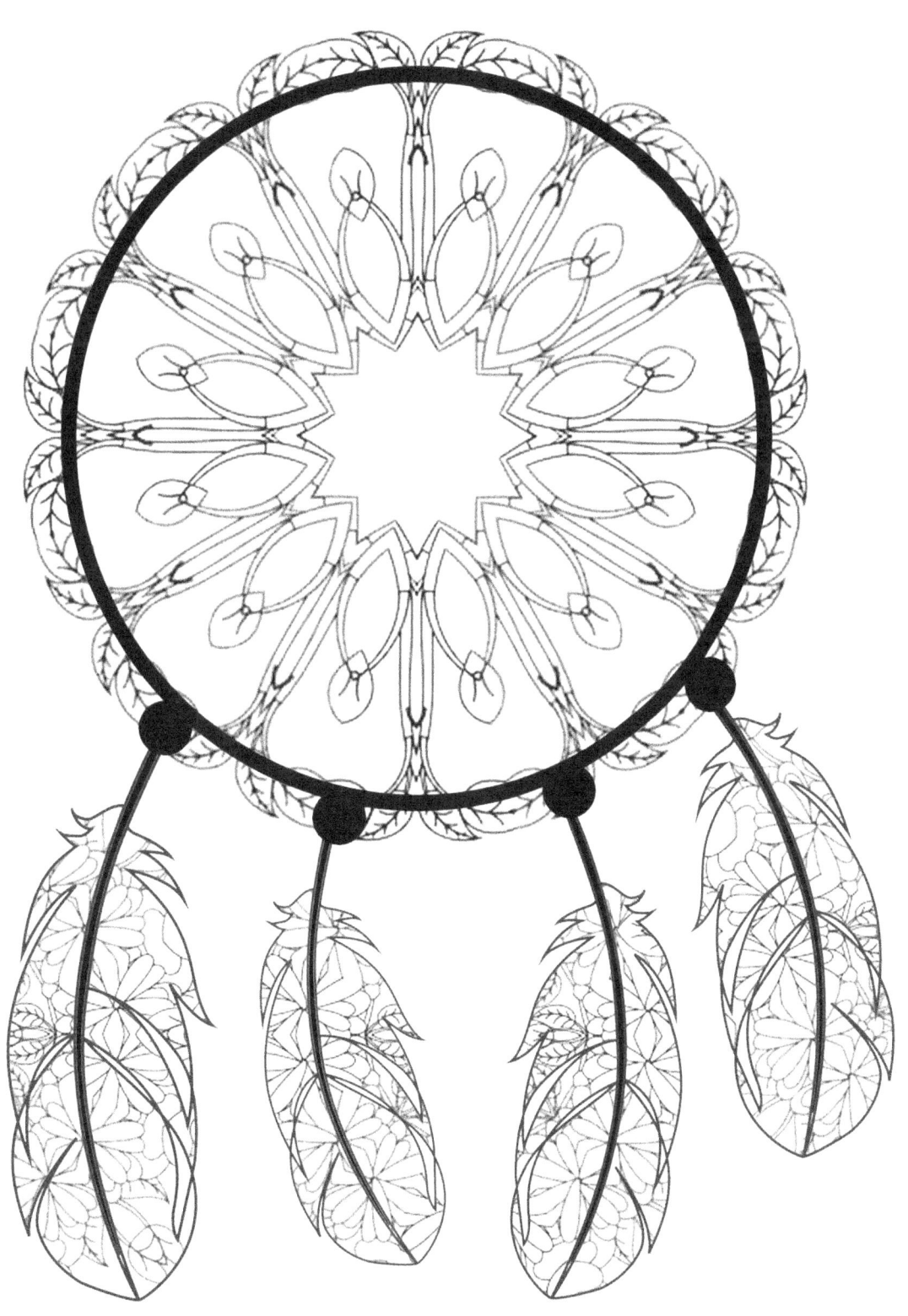

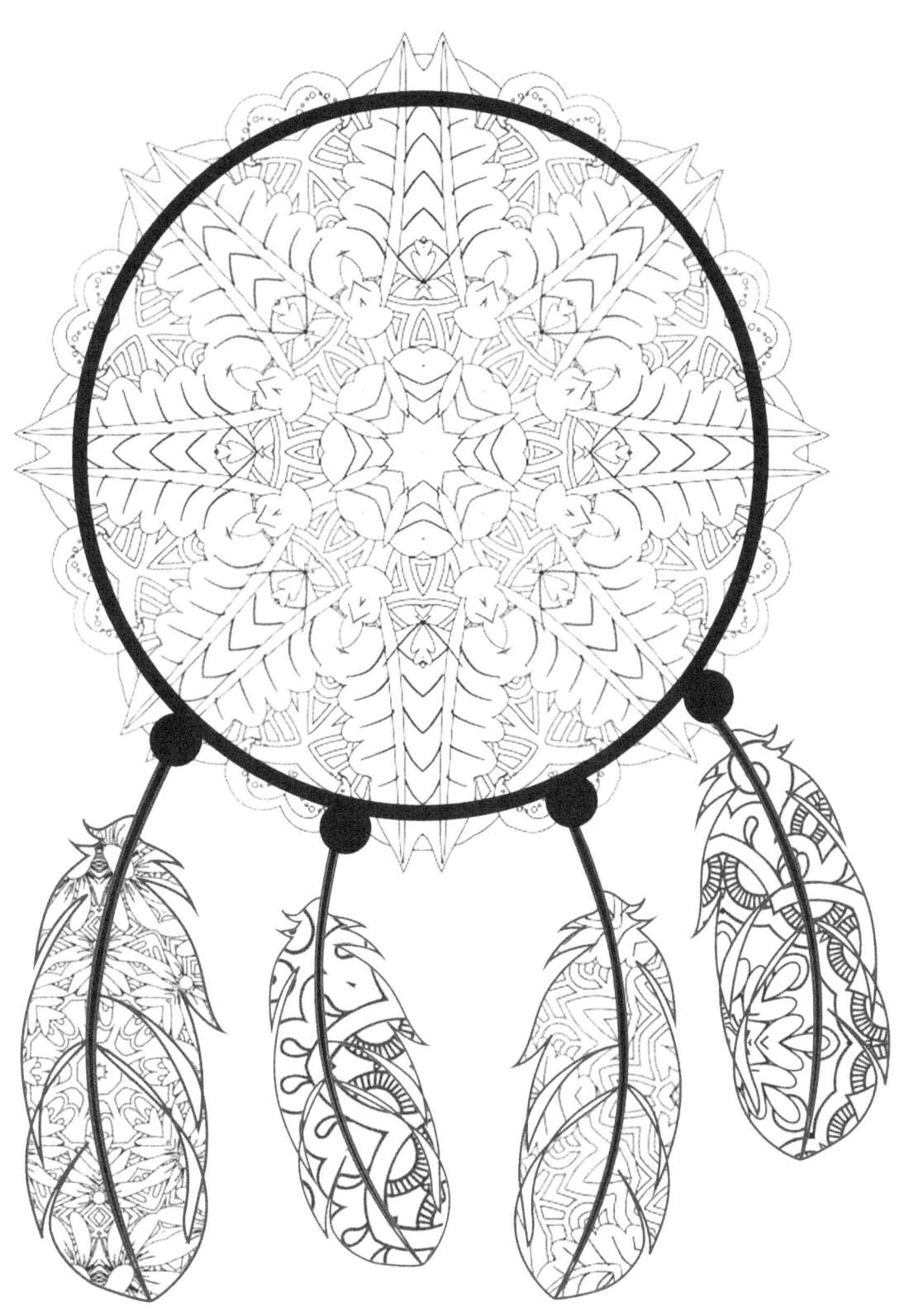

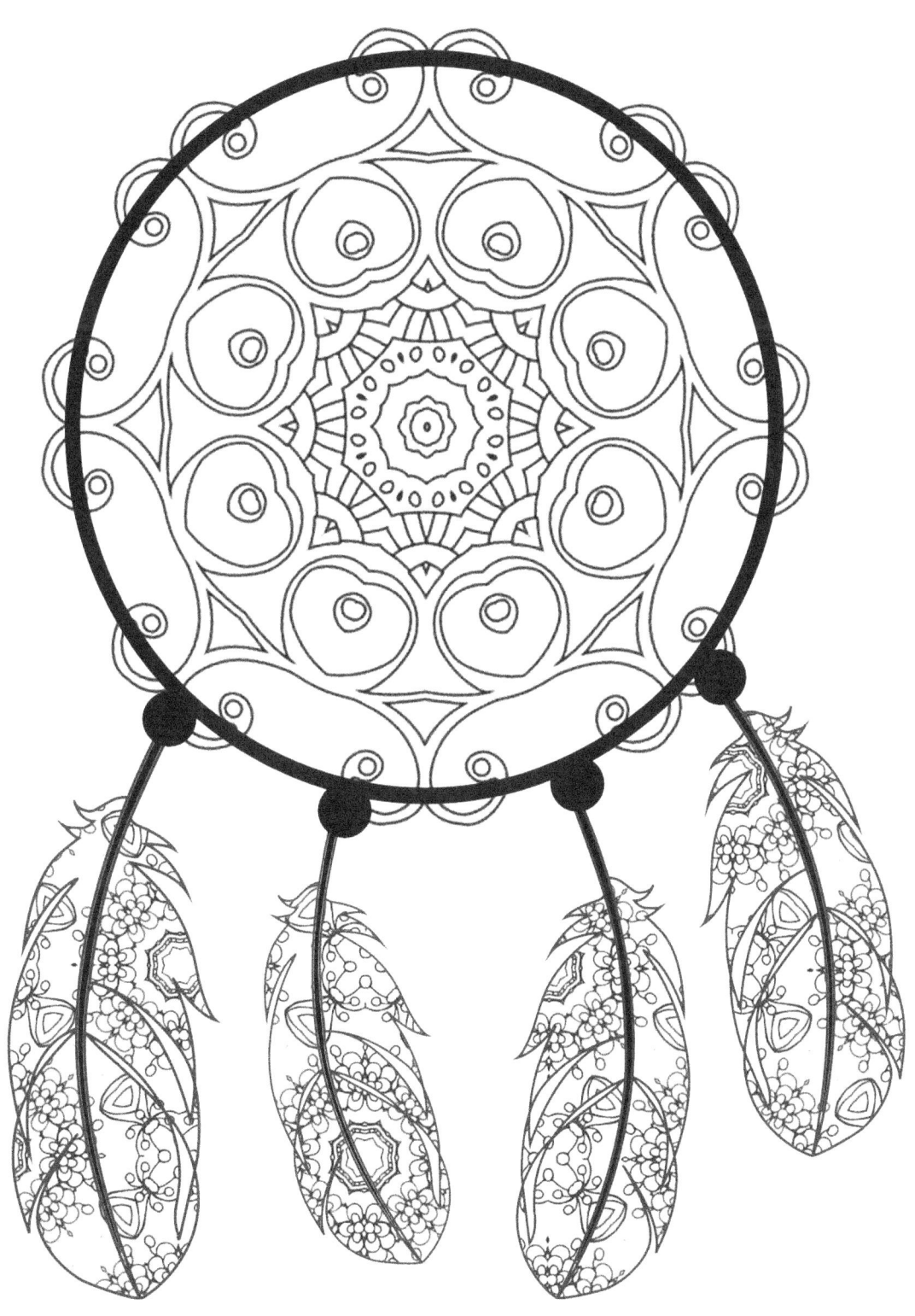

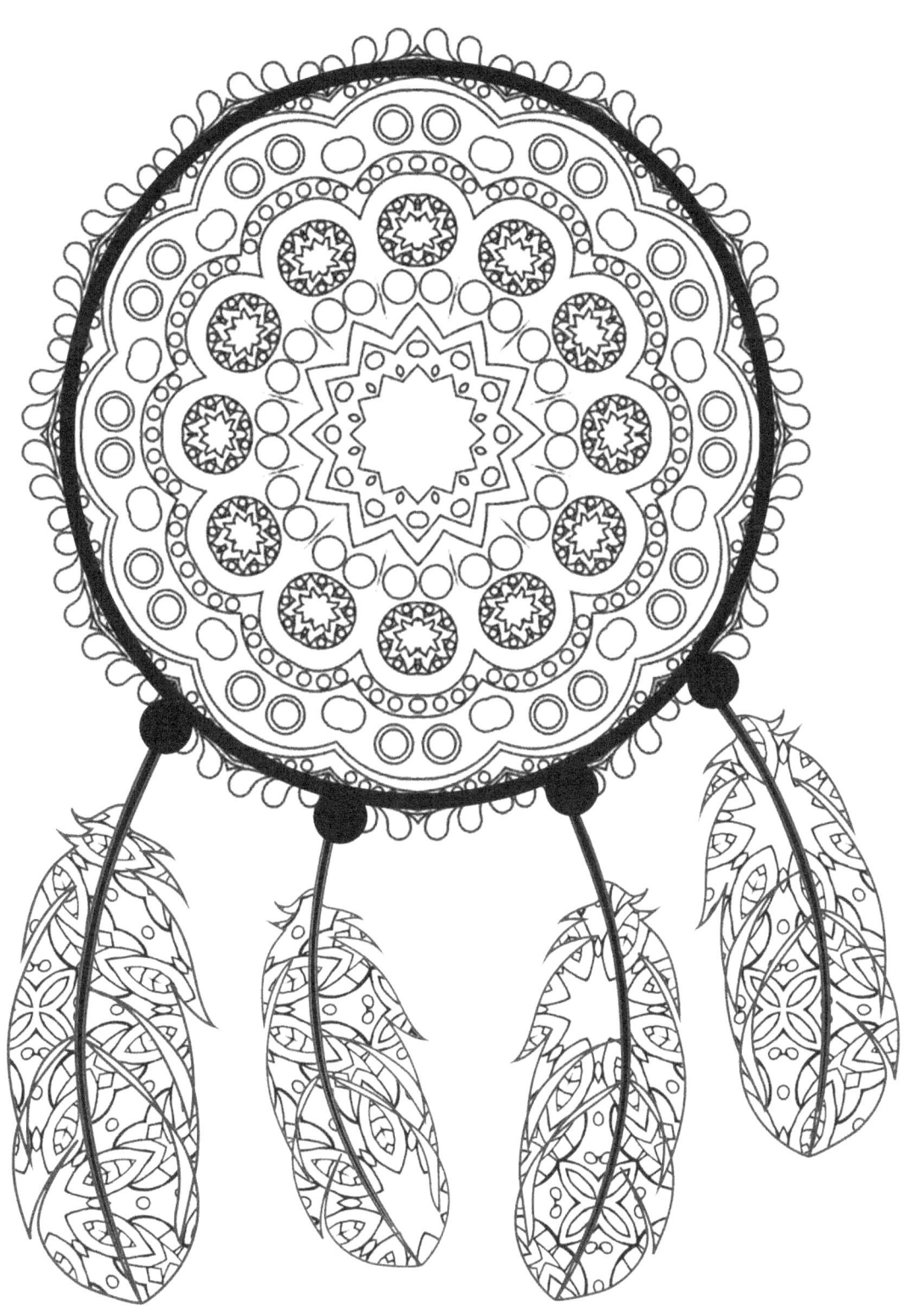

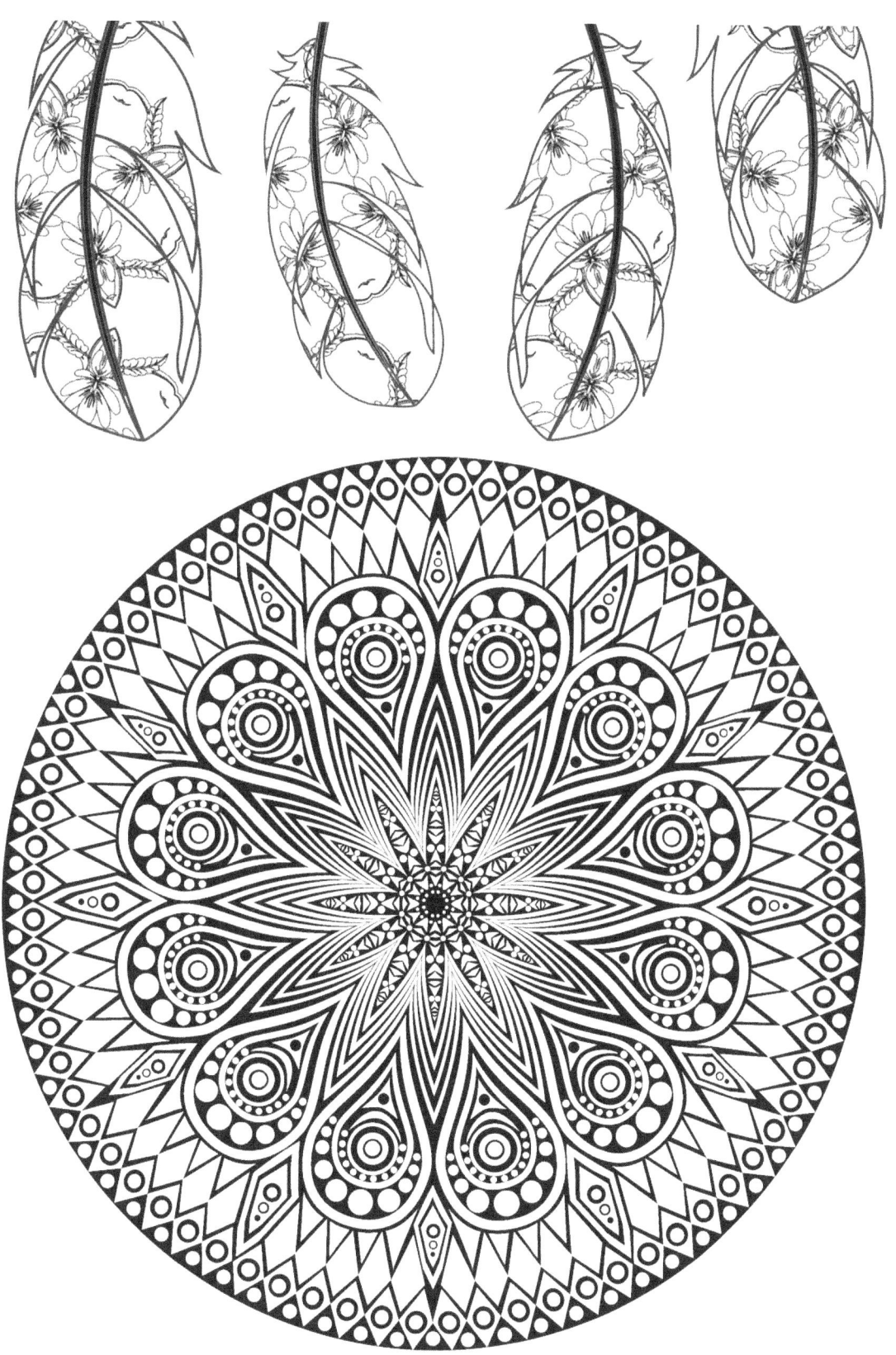

www.ingramcontent.com/pod-product-compliance
Lightning Source LLC
Chambersburg PA
CBHW080553190526
45169CB00007B/2750